AIR PUBLICATION **1564**B & D

Pilot's Notes

PILOT'S NOTES

HURRICANE IIA, IIB, IIC, IID AND IV AIRCRAFT

MERLIN XX ENGINE

Prepared by direction of the
Minister of Aircraft Production

A. C. Rowlands

Promulgated by order of the Air Council

AIR MINISTRY

©2012 Periscope Film LLC
All Rights Reserved
ISBN#978-1-937684-75-4

AIR PUBLICATION ....

Volume I

Pilot's Notes

AMENDMENT CERTIFICATE

Incorporation of an amendment list in this publication should be certified by inserting the amendment list number, initialling in the appropriate column and inserting the date of incorporation.

Holders of the Pilot's Notes will receive only those amendment lists applicable to the Preliminary Matter, and Sections 1 and 2.

Amendt. List No.										
Prelimy. matter										
Leading Partics.										
Introducn.										
Section 1										
Section 2										
Section 3										
Section 4										
Section 5										
Section 6										
Section 7										
Section 8										
Section 9										
Section 10										
Section 11										
Date of incorpn.										

NOTES TO OFFICIAL USERS

Air Ministry Orders and Vol. II leaflets as issued from time to time may affect the subject matter of this publication. It should be understood that amendment lists are not always issued to bring the publication into line with the orders or leaflets and it is for holders of this book to arrange the necessary link-up.

Where an order or leaflet contradicts any portion of this publication, an amendment list will generally be issued, but when this is not done, the order or leaflet must be taken as the **over**riding authority.

Where amendment action has taken place, the number of the amendment list concerned will be found at the top of each page affected, and amendments of technical importance will be indicated by a vertical line on the left-hand side of the text against the matter amended or added. Vertical lines relating to previous amendments to a page are not repeated. If complete revision of any division of the book (e.g. a Chapter) is made this will be indicated in the title page for that division and the vertical lines will not be employed.

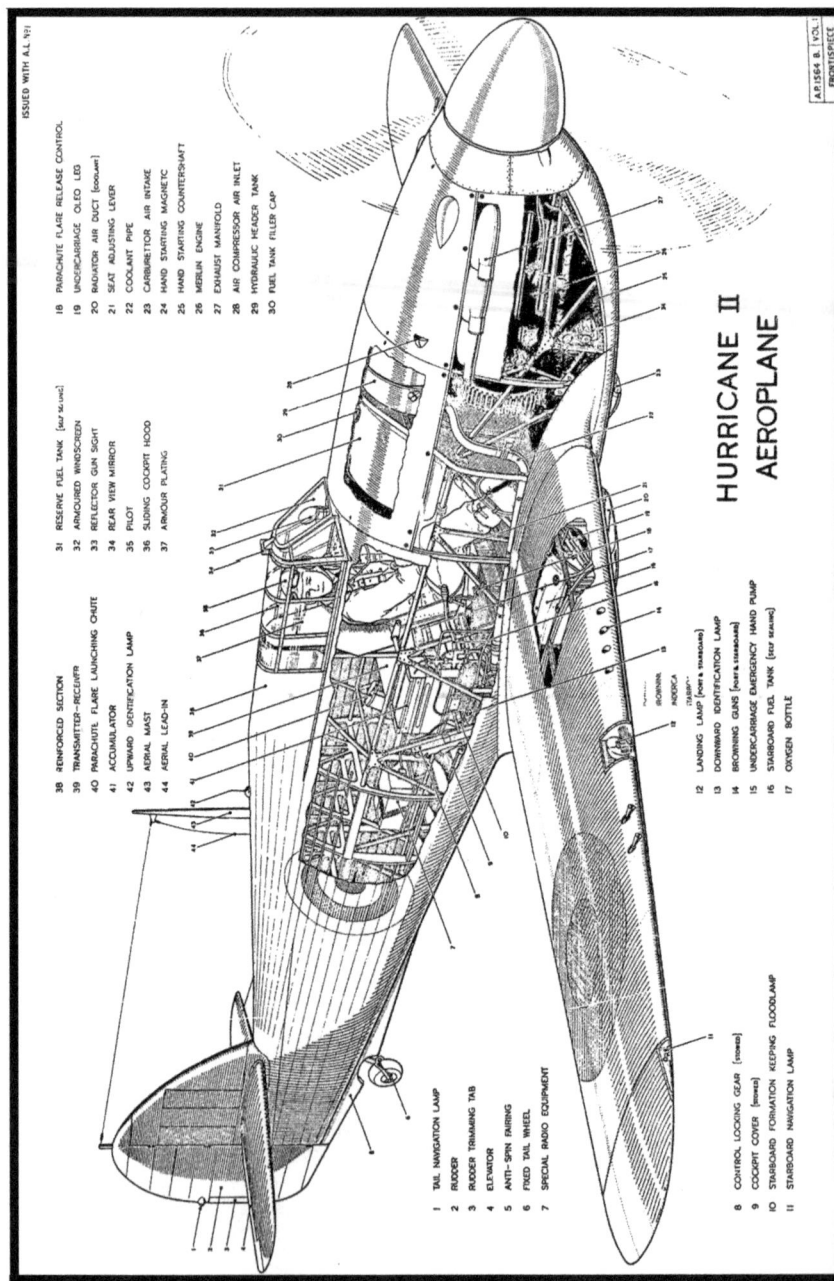

December 1940   AIR PUBLICATION 1564B
                                 Pilot's Notes

LIST OF SECTIONS

(A detailed Contents List appears at
the beginning of each Section)

Introduction:

Section 1.   Controls and equipment for pilot.

Section 2.   Handling and flying notes for pilot.

R.T.P./722. 4500. 12/40.

Revised in Vol. I by A.L.42
and in Pilot's Notes by A.L/P.

AIR PUBLICATION 1564B & D
Volume I and Pilot's Notes.

SECTION I

PILOT'S CONTROLS AND EQUIPMENT

LIST OF CONTENTS

	Para.
INTRODUCTION	1
FUEL, OIL AND COOLANT SYSTEMS	
Fuel tanks	2
Fuel cocks	3
Fuel contents gauge	4
Fuel pressure warning light	5
Oil system	6
Coolant system	7
MAIN SERVICES	
Hydraulic system	8
Electrical system	9
Pneumatic system	10
AIRCRAFT CONTROLS	
Flying controls	11
Trimming tabs	12
Undercarriage and flap control	13
Undercarriage indicators	14
Undercarriage warning light	15
Flap indicator	16
Wheel brakes	17
Flying control locking gear	18
ENGINE CONTROLS	
Throttle	19
Boost control cut-out	20
Propeller control	21
Supercharger control	22
Radiator flap control	23
Slow-running cut-out	24
Cylinder priming pump	25
Engine starting	26
Oil dilution	27
OPERATIONAL EQUIPMENT AND CONTROLS	
Gun controls	28
R.P. controls	29
Bomb controls	30
S.C.I. controls	31
Camera gun control	32
OTHER CONTROLS	
Landing lamps	33
Recognition device	34
EMERGENCIES	
Undercarriage emergency operation	35
Hood jettisoning	36
Emergency exit panel	37
Abandoning by parachute	38
Forced landing	39
Ditching	40
First-aid outfit	41
Crowbar	42

ILLUSTRATIONS

	Fig.
Cockpit - port side	1
Instrument panel	2
Cockpit - starboard side	3
Fig. 4 deleted	
Fuel system diagram - with fixed long-range tanks	5
Fuel system diagram - with jettisonable long-range tanks	5A

Revised in Vol. I by A.L.42
and in Pilot's Notes by A.L/P.

A.P. 1564B & D SECT. 1.
Volume I and Pilot's Notes.

INTRODUCTION

1. The Hurricane Mks. II and IV are each fitted with a Merlin 20 engine and a Rotol 35° propeller. The Mks. IID and IV are low-level attack versions of the earlier Marks and are equipped to carry various alternative armaments. The aircraft controls including the undercarriage, flaps and brakes are identical with those on Mark I aircraft.

FUEL, OIL AND COOLANT SYSTEMS

2. **Fuel tanks** (See Fig. 5 and 5A)

    (i) **Main and Reserve tanks** - The main tanks are housed within the centre section, one on each side of the fuselage, and a reserve tank is carried between the fireproof bulkhead and the instrument panel. Fuel is delivered to the engine by an engine-driven pump. These tanks are self-sealing and their effective capacities are as follows:

Main tanks:	33 gallons each
Reserve tank:	28 gallons

    To meet the possibility of engine cutting due to fuel boiling in warm weather at high altitudes, these tanks can be pressurised (operative above 20,000 feet). Pressurising, however, impairs the self-sealing of tanks and should, therefore, be used only when the fuel pressure warning light comes on, or when auxiliary drop tanks are used (see below).

    (ii) **Auxiliary tanks**: When not fitted with underwing armament or containers, a pair of auxiliary tanks may be carried one under each wing. The types of tank and their capacities are as follows:

Fixed:	44 gallons each
Drop:	45 or 90 gallons each

    With the exception of some fixed tanks which are used for combat duties, these tanks are non-self-sealing. Fuel in the fixed tanks is delivered to the main tanks by electrically driven emmersed pumps, but fuel in the drop tanks is supplied direct to the engine fuel pump by air pressure.

Fuel cocks:

(i) The main fuel cock control (48) on the left-hand side of the cockpit has a spring safety plate which prevents the fuel supply being turned off inadvertently. The control can only be turned to the OFF position whilst the safety plate is held depressed.

(ii) A switch for the electric pump in each fixed auxiliary tank is fitted on the left-hand side of the cockpit, either just above the elevator trimming tab control, or on the lower part of the electrical panel.

(iii) The fuel cock control (73) and jettison lever (74) for the drop tanks are mounted together on the right-hand side of the cockpit, below the windscreen de-icing pump. The cock control has three positions: OFF, PORT and STARBOARD. The pressurising cock must be turned on when the tanks are used. The jettison lever is pulled down to jettison both tanks simultaneously, but cannot be moved until the fuel cock is set to OFF. When the lever is operated, the air pressure supply is automatically cut off.

(iv) The tank pressurising cock (22) is fitted on the left-hand side of the cockpit, below the throttle quadrant, and is marked ATMOSPHERE and PRESSURE.

Fuel contents gauge: A gauge (49) on the right-hand side of the instrument panel indicates selectively the contents of each of the three main tanks. A switch unit (48), comprising a combined selector and pushbutton, is fitted above the gauge.

Fuel pressure warning light: The warning light (50) on the right-hand side of the instrument panel comes on if the pressure drops to 6lb./sq.in.

Oil system: The self-sealing oil tank, which has an effective capacity of 9 gallons, forms the port leading edge of the centre section. The oil passes through a filter before entering the engine and then through a cooler insider the coolant radiator. Pressure (54) and temperature (53) gauges are fitted on the instrument panel. When 90 gallon fuel drop tanks are carried, an auxiliary oil tank of 4 gallons capacity is fitted behind the seat, the cock control for which is on the left-hand side of the seat, above the radiator flap control quadrant.

Revised in Vol. I by A.L.42 A.P. 1564B & D Sect. 1.
and in Pilot's Notes by A.L/P. Volume I and Pilot's Notes.

7. **Coolant system**: The system is thermostatically controlled, the radiator being by-passed until the coolant reaches a certain temperature. The header tank is mounted on the fireproof bulkhead and is fitted with a pressure relief valve. The air flow through the radiator is controlled by a flap lever in the cockpit.

   MAIN SERVICES

8. **Hydraulic system**: An engine-driven hydraulic pump supplies the power for operating the under-carriage and flaps. The system is automatic, selection of the desired operation of the undercarriage or flaps, by means of the selector lever, being sufficient to commence the operation. A handpump (71) is provided for use in the event of engine failure or engine driven pump failure.

9. **Electrical system**: A 12-volt generator, controlled by a switch (3) on the left-hand side of the cockpit, supplies an accumulator which in turn supplies the whole of the electrical installation. There is a voltmeter (31) on the left-hand side of the cockpit, and a red light (36) marked POWER FAILURE on the instrument panel comes on when the generator is not charging the accumulator.

10. **Pneumatic system**: The wheel brakes and the gun-firing mechanism are operated pneumatically, air being supplied by an engine-driven compressor and stored in a cylinder at a maximum pressure of 300 lb./sq.in.

    AIRCRAFT CONTROLS

11. **Flying controls**: The control column is of the spade-grip pattern and incorporates a gun-firing pushbutton and the brake lever. The rudder bar is adjustable for leg reach by means of a starwheel midway between the two pedals.

12. **Trimming tabs**: The elevator trimming tabs are controlled by a handwheel (24) on the left-hand side of the cockpit and an indicator is fitted next to it. Forward rotation of the hand-wheel corrects tail heaviness. The automatic balance tab on the rudder can be set for trimming purposes by means of a small control wheel (23) on the left-hand side of the cockpit which is turned clockwise to apply right rudder.

13. **Undercarriage and flap control**: The selector lever (76) for the undercarriage and flaps is on the right-hand side of the cockpit and works in a gate, having a neutral position for both undercarriage and flaps, the positions for operating the flaps being outboard. The catch on the side of the lever must be pressed in order to release it for movement from an

operative position, but the lever can be moved from the neutral position without first releasing the catch. To obviate inadvertent selection on the ground of the wheels up position, a safety catch (77) is provided on the gate which must be turned in a clockwise direction to permit entry of the selector lever into the wheels UP slot. For emergency lowering of the undercarriage see Para. 35.

14. Undercarriage indicator: The electrical indicator (41) is on the left-hand side of the instrument panel and has duplicate pairs of lamps, the green lamps indicating when the undercarriage is locked in the DOWN position and the red lamps when the undercarriage is fully retracted and locked. There are two switches to the left of the indicator, the left-hand one (38) being the ON-OFF switch for the green lamps, and the right-hand one (39) being the change-over switch for the duplicate sets of lamps. A dimmer switch is provided in the centre of the indicator. When the undercarriage is retracted, the wheels are visible through two small windows in the bottom of the cockpit.

15. Undercarriage warning light: A red light on the instrument panel comes on at any time when the throttle lever is less than one third open and the undercarriage is not locked down. When the throttle is opened again or the undercarriage is lowered the light goes out.

16. Flap indicator: This (72) is mechanically operated, the pointer moving along a graduated scale marked UP and DOWN at its extremities. It is situated immediately below the hydraulic selector lever.

17. Wheel brakes: The brake lever is fitted on the control column spade-grip and a catch for retaining it in the on position for parking is fitted below the lever pivot. A triple pressure gauge, showing the air-pressure in the pneumatic system cylinder and at each brake, is mounted forward of the foot of the control column.

18. Flying control locking gear: The locking struts, interference bar and bracket are stowed in a canvas bag in the starboard side of the wireless bay. The bracket clips on to the control

column, just below the spade grip, for locking of the
aileron control and the two struts, attached to the
bracket by shackles, lock the rudder bar and control
column. The spring loaded interference bar fits on to
the bracket and is inserted in a slot in the back of the
seat.

ENGINE CONTROLS

19. Throttle: The throttle lever (7) works in a slot in
the decking shelf on the left-hand side of the cockpit.
The take-off position is gated. There is a friction
adjuster (16) on the inboard end of the lever spindle.
The mixture control is fully automatic and there is no
pilot's control lever.

20. Boost control cut-out: The automatic boost control may
be cut out by pulling the knob (34) on the left-hand
side of the instrument panel.

21. Propeller control: The speed control lever (10) on the
left-hand side of the cockpit varies the governed rpm
from 3,000 down to 1,800. A friction adjuster is fitted
on the inboard side of the control.

22. Supercharger control: The push-pull control (17) is fitted
below the left-hand side of the instrument panel, and must
be pushed in for low (M) gear and pulled out for high (S)
gear

23. Radiator flap control: The airflow through the coolant
radiator and oil cooler is controlled by a lever (26) on
the left-hand side of the pilot's seat. In order to
release the lever for operation the thumb-button must be
depressed.

24. Slow-running cut-out: The control on the carburettor is
operated by pulling out the knob (64) immediately to the
right of the undercarriage and flap selector lever.

25. Cylinder priming pump: The priming pump (59) is fitted
below the right-hand side of the instrument panel.

26. **Engine starting**: The starter and booster coil push-buttons (32 & 33) are to the left of the ignition switches (58) on the instrument panel. An external supply socket for the starter motor is accessible through a removable panel in the starboard engine cowling, and two handles for hand starting are stowed in the undercarriage wheel recess under the centre section.

27. **Oil dilution**: The pushbutton (4) for operating the solenoid valve is on the left-hand side of the cockpit.

    OTHER CONTROLS

28. **Gun controls**: The machine guns and cannon are normally fired by the pushbutton on the control column spade grip. The two 40 m.m. guns on MK IID and IV aircraft are fired electro-pneumatically by the pushbutton in the throttle lever; they cannot be fired, however, until the master switch (11) on the decking shelf, forward of the throttle quadrant, is switched on. The cocking lever (28) on the electrical panel to the left of the seat should be pushed down in the event of a misfire.

29. **R.P. controls**: The projectiles are fired by the pushbutton in the throttle lever and a selector switch (40) below the left-hand side of the windscreen enables them to be fired in PAIRS or as a SALVO. They must not be fired with the flaps lowered.

30. **Bomb controls**: There are two selector switches and two nose and tail fusing switches on a small panel (67) on the right-hand side of the cockpit. The bombs are released by the pushbutton in the throttle lever.

31. **S.C.I. controls**: These are operated by the pushbutton in the throttle lever and there is a container jettison push-button (63) on the right-hand side of the cockpit.

32. **Camera gun control**: The camera gun operates only when the guns and cannon or the R.P. are fired, or when the lower pushbutton on the control column spade grip is depressed.

Revised in Vol. I by A.L.42. A.P.1564B & D Sect. 1.
and in Pilot's Notes by A.L/P. Volume I and Pilot's Notes.

33. <u>Landing lamps</u>: The landing lamps, one in the leading edge of each wing, are controlled by a two-way switch (15) to the left of the instrument panel, which enables either lamp to be used; both lamps are off when the switch is in the upright position. A dipping lever (5) on the left-hand side of the cockpit can be held in any position by tightening the knurled wheel; when the wheel is unscrewed, the lever is pulled aft into the UP position by a return spring in each of the lamp units.

34. <u>Recognition device</u>: The flares are selected and released by a single lever (25) immediately aft of the trimming tab control The slot is marked SELECT and FIRE.

    EMERGENCIES

35. <u>Undercarriage emergency operation</u>:

    (i) In the event of failure of the engine-driven hydraulic pump, the undercarriage may be lowered by moving the selector lever to the WHEELS DOWN position and then operating the handpump.

    (ii) If the handpump fails to lower the undercarriage the selector lever should still be left in the WHEELS DOWN position and the red-painted foot pedal (21), outboard of the port heelrest, should be firmly pushed forward. The wheels should then fall and lock down under their own weight.

    (iii) If difficulty is experienced in operating the undercarriage and flap selector lever it may be overcome by first selecting the opposite to that which is required. If, for example, the selection of undercarriage down is found to be difficult, the lever should first be moved into the undercarriage up position and then immediately moved to the down position.

36. <u>Hood jettisoning</u>: To jettison the hood the lever aft of the radiator flap control should be pulled sharply forward and upwards. If the hood does not readily leave the aircraft it should be assisted by pushing it upwards, or failing that, by releasing the emergency exit panel (see below) in addition to operating the jettison control.

    <u>Note</u>: When jettisoning the hood it is advisable to lower one's head as far as possible so as to avoid injury when it leaves the aircraft.

37. **Emergency exit panel**: The large detachable panel on the starboard side of the cockpit is secured by horizontal spring-loaded plungers and a bolt operated by the cockpit hood. To jettison the panel, the hood must first be fully opened and the release lever (66) then moved aft and upwards.

38. **Abandoning by parachute**: When abandoning the aircraft by parachute it is important to decrease speed and then dive over the side immediately. The pilot must not stand on the seat and delay in jumping or he will hit either the aerial mast or the tailplane.

39. **Forced landing**: In the event of having to make a forced landing the glide may be lengthened considerably by moving the propeller speed control fully back and gliding at about 130 mph IAS. With undercarriage and flaps up the gliding angle at speeds of 120-140 mph IAS is very flat.

40. **Ditching** (See A.P.2095 Pilot's Notes General)

    (i) In general the pilot should, if possible, abandon the aircraft by parachute.

    (ii) In the event of having to ditch, auxiliary drop tanks, bombs or containers (if fitted) should be jettisoned and the following procedure should be observed:

    (a) The cockpit hood should be jettisoned

    (b) Flaps should be lowered fully in order to reduce landing speed as much as possible

    (c) The undercarriage should be retracted

    (d) Safety harness should be kept on, with straps tight, and the R/T plug disconnected

    (e) The engine, if available, should be used to help make the touch-down in a tail-down attitude at as low a speed as possible

    (f) When about to touch the water a normal banked turn, with full rudder, should be made so as to prevent 'hooking' the radiator into the water

Revised in Vol. I by A.L.42　　　A.P. 1564B & D Sect. 1.
and in Pilot's Notes by A.L/P　　Volume I and Pilot's Notes.

41. **First-aid outfit**: The first-aid outfit is attached to the inside of a detachable panel on the port side of the cockpit and is accessible by kicking in the panel breaking the stringers, and tearing the fabric.

42. **Crowbar**: A crowbar, for use in an emergency, is stowed in clips to the right of the seat.

KEY TO FIG. 1

1. Radio contactor master switch
2. Cockpit light dimmer switch
3. Generator switch
4. Oil dilution pushbutton
5. Landing lamp control lever
6. Oxygen supply cock
7. Throttle lever (incorporating pushbutton)
8. Socket for footage indicator plug
9. Wedge plate for camera gun footage indicator
10. Propeller speed control
11. Cannon master switch
12. Compass light dimmer switch
13. Cockpit light
14. Cockpit light dimmer switch
15. Landing lamp switch
16. Friction adjuster
17. Supercharger control
18. Fuel cock control
19. R.T.9D contactor switch
20. Radio contactor
21. Undercarriage emergency release lever
22. Fuel tank pressurising control
23. Rudder trimming tab control
24. Elevator trimming tab control
25. Recognition device selector lever
26. Radiator flap control lever
27. Heated clothing socket
28. Cannon cocking lever
29. Microphone/telephone socket
30. Hood catch control
31. Voltmeter

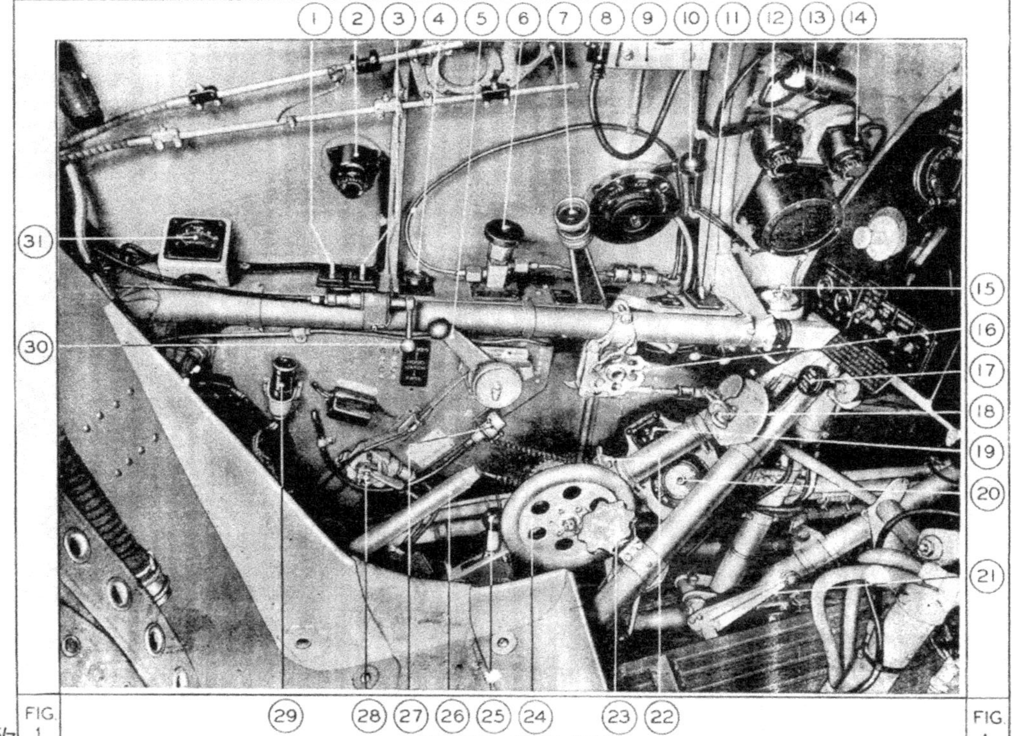

FIG. 1 COCKPIT - PORT SIDE

Revised in Vol. I by A.L.42
and in Pilot's Notes by A.L/P

KEY TO FIG. 2

32. Engine starter pushbutton
33. Booster coil pushbutton
34. Boost control cut-out
35. Oxygen regulator
36. Power failure warning light
37. Cockpit ventilator
38. Undercarriage indicator ON-OFF switch
39. Undercarriage indicator change-over switch
40. R.P. selector switch
41. Undercarriage indicator
42. Instrument flying panel.
43. Reflector sight spare lamps
44. Engine speed indicator
45. Reflector sight switch
46. Cockpit ventilator
47. Boost gauge
48. Fuel contents gauge selector switch
49. Fuel contents gauge
50. Fuel pressure warning light
51. Radiator temperature gauge
52. Beam approach master switch
53. Beam approach master switch
54. Oil pressure gauge
55. Camera gun switch
56. Navigation lights switch
57. Pressure head heater switch
58. Ignition switches

A.P. 1564 B & D VOL I & P.N. SECT. I

INSTRUMENT PANEL

FIG. 2

KEY TO FIG. 3

59. Cylinder priming pump
60. Cockpit light
61. Cockpit light dimmer switch
62. Signalling switch box
63. Container jettison pushbutton
64. Slow-running cut-out
65. Windscreen de-icing pump
66. Emergency exit panel jettison lever
67. Bomb fusing and selector switches
68. Sutton harness release
69. I.F.F. master switch
70. I.F.F. pushbuttons
71. Hydraulic handpump
72. Flap indicator
73. Drop tank fuel cock control
74. Drop tank jettison control
75. Seat adjustment lever
76. Undercarriage and flap selector lever
77. Undercarriage selector safety catch

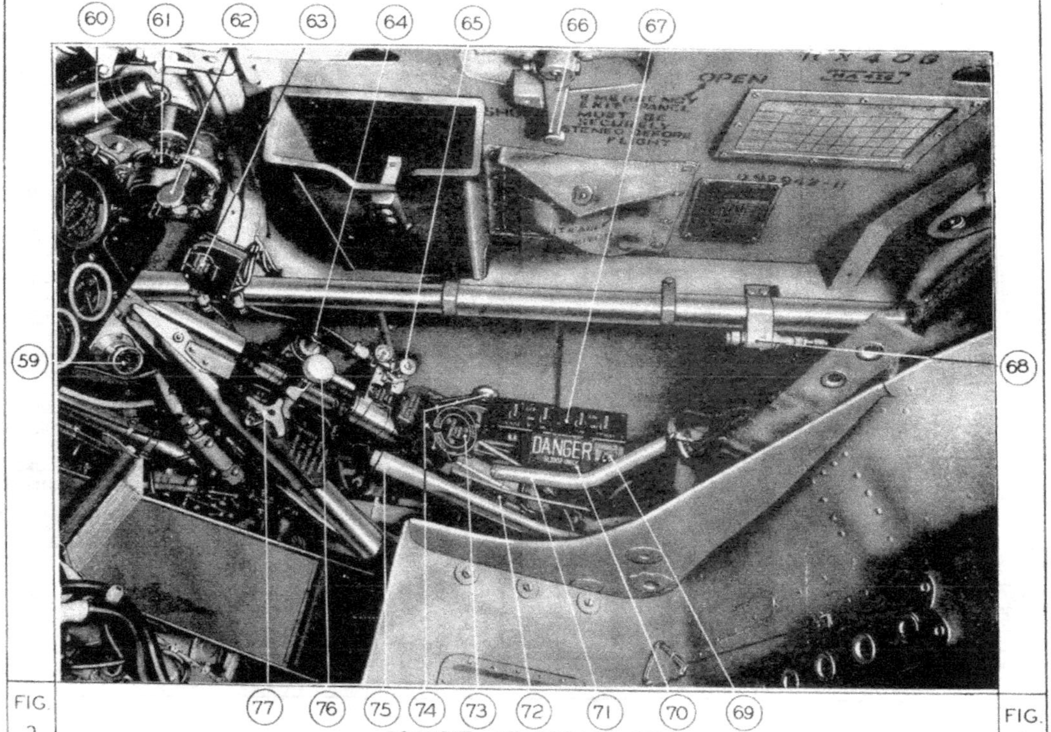

FIG. 3

COCKPIT - STARBOARD SIDE

FIG. 3

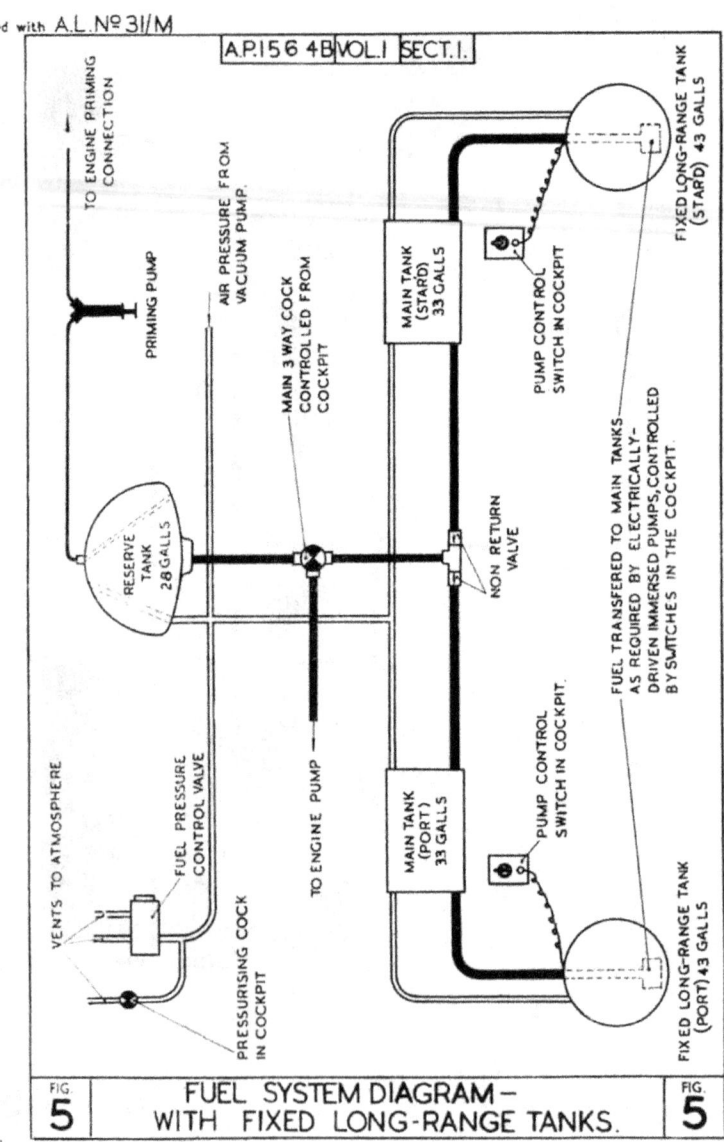

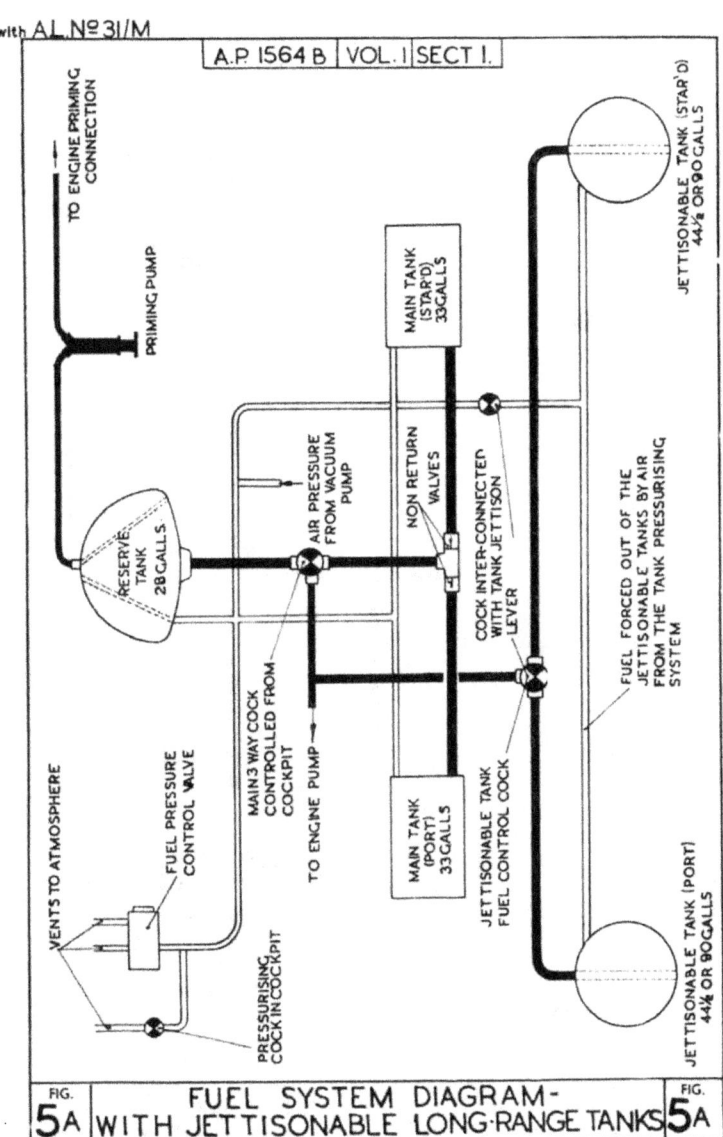

FIG. 5A — FUEL SYSTEM DIAGRAM — WITH JETTISONABLE LONG-RANGE TANKS

AIR PUBLICATION 1564B + D
VOLUME I AND PILOTS NOTES

SECTION 2
Handling and Flying Notes

1. Engine Data
2. Flying Limitations
3. Position Error Corrections
4. Management of Fuel and Oil Systems
5. Preliminaries
6. Starting the Engine and Warming Up
7. Testing the Engine and Installations
8. Check List before Take-Off
9. Take-Off
10. Climbing
11. General Flying
12. Maximum Performance
13. Economical Flying
14. Stalling
15. Spinning
16. Aerobatics
17. Diving
18. Check List before Landing
19. Approach and Landing
20. Mislanding
21. After Landing
22. Fuel Capacities and Consumption
23. Beam Approach

Revised in Vol. I by A.L.42
and in Pilot's Notes by A.L./P.

AIR PUBLICATION 1564B & D
Volume I and Pilot's Notes.

SECTION 2

HANDLING AND FLYING NOTES FOR PILOT

1. ENGINE DATA: MERLIN XX

    (i) **Fuel:** 100 octane only

    (ii) **Oil:** See A.P. 1464/C.37

    (iii) Engine limitations:

		R.p.m.	Boost lb./sq.in.	Temp. $^{\circ}$C Clnt.	Oil
MAX. TAKE-OFF TO 1,000 FEET	M	3,000	+12	-	-
MAX. CLIMBING 1 HR. LIMIT	M) S)	2,850	+9	125	90
MAX. RICH CONTINUOUS	M) S)	2,650	+7	105‡	90
MAX. WEAK CONTINUOUS	M) S)	2,650	+4	105‡	90
COMBAT 5 MINS. LIMIT	M S	3,000 3,000	+14* +16*	135 135	105 105

    Note:

    * Combat boost is obtained by operating the boost control cut-out.

    $\ddagger$ 115°C coolant temperature is permitted for short periods at cruising rpm.

OIL PRESSURE:	NORMAL:	60-80 lb./sq.in.
	MINIMUM:	45
MINM. TEMP. FOR TAKE-OFF:	OIL:	15°C
	COOLANT:	60°C
FUEL PRESSURE:		8-10 lb./sq.in.

2. FLYING LIMITATIONS

   (i) <u>Maximum speeds (mph IAS)</u>:

Diving:	390
Undercarriage down:	120
Flaps down:	120

   (ii) At AUWs in excess of 8,750 lb. care is necessary in ground handling and the aircraft should be taken off only from concrete or equivalent runways.

   (iii) Spinning is probibited at all times of Mark IID and IV aircraft, and of Mark IIA, B and C aircraft only when carrying 90-gallon drop tanks, bombs, SCI, containers, or RP.

   (iv) Aerobatics are prohibited and violent manoeuvres must be avoided when carrying 90-gallon drop tanks, bombs, SCI, containers, or RP (Mk IIA, B and C aircraft only).

   (v) Aircraft carrying drop tanks should not be dived.

   (vi) Mark III containers must not be dropped at speeds in excess of 150 mph IAS and at heights lower than 500 feet.

   (vii) Bombs should be jettisoned and RP fired, if possible, before landing.

3. POSITION ERROR CORRECTIONS

From	100	120	150	180	210	270	mph IAS
To	120	150	180	210	270	320	mph IAS
Add	4	2	0				mph
Subtract			0	2	4	6	mph

4. MANAGEMENT OF FUEL AND OIL SYSTEMS

   (i) The Main Tanks should be used first, but if the Reserve Tank is used before the Main Tanks, the following precautions must be observed:

   (a) Change over to MAIN TANKS ON before emptying the Reserve Tank.

   (b) If this has not been done and the engine cuts, close the throttle (to avoid over-revving when the engine picks up) and change over to MAIN TANKS ON <u>at once</u>.

Revised in Vol. I by A.L.42 A.P. 1564B & D Sect. 2
and in Pilot's Notes by A.L/P. Volume I and Pilot's Notes.

- (c) In order to displace air drawn into the fuel system from the empty reserve tank, the engine must be windmilled at high speed, when it will pick up after a few seconds. It is emphasised that the pick-up will not be immediate after the change-over.

(ii) If fitted with fixed auxiliary tanks:

- (a) Start and take-off in the normal way on the main tanks.

- (b) As soon as the contents gauge registers only 5 gallons in the main tanks, switch ON the auxiliary tank pumps.

- (c) Switch OFF the pumps immediately the contents gauge registers 25 gallons.

- (d) When the contents of the MAIN TANKS are again reduced to 5 gallons, switch ON the pumps until the contents gauge again registers 25 gallons and then switch OFF the pumps. The auxiliary tanks will then be practically empty.

(iii) If fitted with drop tanks:

- (a) Start and take-off in the normal way on the main tanks.

- (b) At a safe height (say 2,000 feet) change over to a drop tank and turn the pressurising cock to PRESSURE. Turn OFF the main tanks.

- (c) When the drop tank is empty and the fuel pressure warning light comes on, change-over to the second drop tank and at the same time turn ON the reserve tank, which should still be full. This will enable the engine to pick up more quickly and when it does so turn OFF the reserve tank and change-over to the second drop tank.

- (d) When the second drop tank is empty and the fuel pressure warning light comes on, turn ON the main tanks and turn OFF the drop tank. If the engine does not pick up on the main tanks, prime the system by using the reserve tank as before.

F.S/2

(e) The cock for the auxiliary oil tank (if fitted) should be turned on about $3\frac{1}{2}$ hours after take-off, but not before this time. After having been turned on, the cock cannot afterwards be turned off during flight.

(f) On reinforcing flights, under maximum range engine conditions (2,650 rpm and +4 lb./sq.in. boost on climb to height, and level flight at 190 mph IAS reducing to 160 mph IAS after jettisoning tanks) oil consumption is considerably reduced and, therefore, the auxiliary oil tank should not be turned on until after approximately 5 hours flight, when there will be sufficient space in the main tank to accommodate the extra 4 gallons. The normal oil tank should be filled to 8 gallons only.

5. PRELIMINARIES

(i) If fitted with R.P. and a drop tank or R.P. and a bomb, the aircraft should be trimmed carefully to relieve stick load.

The recommended aileron tab setting is neutral at full load. Then with a drop tank fitted under the port wing, changes in load will cause the following alterations in trim:

Tank empty:	Slightly right wing low
Tank empty and RP fired:	Trim satisfactory
Tank jettisoned and RP fired:	Slightly right wing low
Tank jettisoned, RP not fired:	Right wing low

(ii) Switch on the undercarriage indicator and check green lights. Test the change-over switch.

(iii) See that the short (lower) arm of the hydraulic selector safety catch is across the wheels up slot of the gate.

(iv) Check that the throttle pushbutton master switch is OFF.

(v) Check contents of fuel tanks. If fitted with auxiliary tanks see that the pump switches or cock control are OFF.

(vi) Test operation of flying controls.

(vii) See that the cockpit hood is locked open.

Revised in Vol. I by A.L.42
and in Pilot's Notes by A.L/P.

A.P. 1564B & D Sect. 2
Volume I and Pilot's Notes.

6. STARTING THE ENGINE AND WARMING UP

   (i) Set fuel cock to MAIN TANKS ON.

   (ii) Set the controls as follows:

       Throttle   - $\frac{1}{2}$ inch open

       Propeler control   - fully forward

       Supercharger control - MODERATE

       Radiator shutter   - OPEN

   (iii) If an external priming connection is fitted, high volatility fuel (Stores Ref. 34A/111) should be used for priming at air temperatures below freezing. Work the priming pump until the fuel reaches the priming nozzles; this may be judged by a sudden increase in resistance.

   (iv) Switch ON the ignition and press the starter and booster coil pushbuttons. Turning periods must not exceed 20 seconds, with a 30 seconds wait between each. Work the priming pump as rapidly and vigorously as possible while the engine is being turned; it should start after the following number of strokes if cold:

Air temperature °C:	+30	+20	+10	0	-10	-20
Normal fuel:	3	4	7	12		
High volatility fuel:				4	8	18

   (v) At temperatures below freezing it will probably be necessary to continue priming after the engine has fired and until it picks up on the carburettor.

   (vi) Release the starter button as soon as the engine starts and as soon as it is running satisfactorily release the booster coil pushbutton and screw down the priming pump.

   (vii) Open up slowly to 1,000 rpm, then warm up at this speed.

7. TESTING THE ENGINE AND INSTALLATIONS

   While warming up:

   (i) Check temperatures and pressures, and test operation of hydraulic system by lowering and raising the flaps.

After warming up, with two men on the tail:

Note: The following tests consitute a comprehensive check to be carried out after inspection or repair, or at the pilot's discretion. In normal circumstances they may be reduced in accordance with local instructions.

(ii) Open up to +4 lb./sq.in. boost and exercise and check operation of the two speed supercharger. Rpm should fall when S ratio is engaged.

(iii) At +4 lb./sq.in. boost exercise and check operation of the constant speed propeller. Rpm should fall to 1,800 with the control fully back. Check that the generator is charging; the power failure light should be out and the voltage 14 or over.

(iv) With the propeller control fully forward open the throttle up to +12 lb./sq.in. boost and check static boost and rpm which should be 3,000.

(v) Throttle back to +9 lb./sq.in. boost and test each magneto in turn. The drop should not exceed 150 rpm.

(vi) Before taxying check brake pressure (100 lb./sq in. minm.) and pneumatic supply pressure (220 lb./sq.in.)

CHECK LIST BEFORE TAKE-OFF

```
T  -  Trimming tabs       -  Rudder: Fully right
                             Elevator: Nautral
P  -  Propeller control   -  Fully forward
F  -  Fuel                -  Check contents of main tanks
                          -  MAIN TANKS ON
                          -  Aux. tank cock or pumps - OFF
                          -  Pressuring cock - ATMOSPHERE
F  -  Flaps               -  UP (28° down - two divs. on
                             indicator - for shortest take-off run)
      Supercharger
      control             -  MODERATE
      Radiator shutter    -  Fully OPEN
```

TAKE-OFF

(i) Open the throttle slowly to the gate, or fully if full take-off boost is necessary.

(ii) Any tendency to swing can be counteracted by the rudder. When fitted with 2 x 500 lb. bombs the tendency to swing left is slightly more pronounced.

Revised in Vol. I by A.L.42 A.P. 1564B & D Sect. 2
and in Pilot's Notes by A.L/P. Volume I and Pilot's Notes.

- (iii) After raising the undercarriage return the selector lever to neutral and retrim nose heavy.
- (iv) Do not start to climb before a speed of 140 mph IAS is attained.

10. CLIMBING

  (i) The speeds for maximum rate of climb are as follows:

Up to 16,000 feet:	140 mph IAS
At 21,000 feet:	135 mph IAS
At 26,000 feet:	130 mph IAS
At 31,000 feet:	125 mph IAS

  Change to S ratio when the boost has fallen by 5 lb./sq.in.
  At full load 155 mph IAS is the most comfortable climbing speed.
  Considerable surging may be experienced above 8,000 feet on aircraft on which the air intake duct has been removed.

  (ii) When fitted with 2 x 90-gallon drop tanks the aircraft are longitudinally unstable on the climb.

  (iii) When fitted with 2 x 500 lb. bombs there is a similar tendency to pitch if the rudder is not held steady.

  (iv) The fuel tank pressure control should normally be kept to ATMOSPHERE (except when required to supply fuel from the drop tanks), but should be turned on (PRESSURE) if the fuel pressure warning light comes on.

11. GENERAL FLYING

  (i) **Stability**: The aircraft are normally just stable longitudinally, but when carrying 90-gallon drop tanks, or R.P. and one 90-gallon drop tank, they become unstable longitudinally and, in the first case, 190 mph IAS is the minimum comfortable flying speed. In conditions of absolute calm this can be reduced to 180 mph IAS. When carrying bombs, R.P. or containers, longitudinal stability is unaffected.

(ii) Change of trim:

        Undercarriage down - Nose slightly down

        Flaps down - Nose down

(iii) In steep turns there is a tendency to tighten up.

(iv) In bad visibility near the ground, flaps should be lowered to about $40°$ (3 divisions) and the propeller speed control set to give 2,650 rpm. Speed may then be reduced to about 110 mph IAS. The radiator shutter must be opened to keep the temperature at about $100°C$.

(v) When operating in tropical conditions prolonged flying at maximum cruising power should be avoided when top speed is not essential.

2. MAXIMUM PERFORMANCE

(i) Climbing:

See Para. 10(i).

(ii) Combat:

Use S ratio if the boost in M ratio is 2 lb./sq.in. below the maximum permitted.

3. ECONOMICAL FLYING

(i) Climbing: Climb at 2,850 rpm and +9 lb./sq.in. boost at the speeds recommended for maximum rate of climb (See Para. 10).

(ii) Cruising: For maximum range fly in M ratio and at maximum obtainable boost not exceeding +4 lb./sq.in. and reduce speed by reducing rpm which may be as low as 1,800, but check that the generator is charging. On some early aircraft it will not do so at below 2,000 rpm. If at 1,800 rpm (or 2,000 if necessary) the speed is higher than that recommended, reduce boost.

S ratio should only be used if at 2,600 rpm the recommended speed cannot be obtained in M ratio.

Revised in Vol. I by A.L.42   A.P. 1564B & D Sect. 2
and in Pilot's Notes by A.L/P.   Volume I and Pilot's Notes.

(iii) The recommended speeds (mph IAS) for maximum range are:

Standard aircraft:	160
When fitted with 2 x 44 or 45 gal. tanks	160
When fitted with 2 x 90 gal. tanks	170 or as near as possible
When fitted with 2 x 250 lb. bombs	170
When fitted with 2 x 500 lb. bombs	180

14. STALLING

(i) At the stall one wing usually drops sharply, often over the vertical, with flaps either up or down.

(ii) The average stalling speeds (mph IAS) for the aircraft at various AUW (from 7,600 lbs. to 9,200 lbs.) are:

Undercarriage and flaps UP:	80-90
Undercarriage and flaps DOWN:	60-75

The speeds for individual aircraft may vary by 5 mph.

15. SPINNING

(i) Spinning of Mk IID and Mk IV aircraft is prohibited at all times.

(ii) On Mark IIA, B and C aircraft spinning is prohibited when carrying 90-gallon drop tanks, bombs, SCI or R.P.

(iii) Recovery is normal, but the loss of height involved in recovery may be very great and the following limits are to be observed:

    (a) Spins are not to be started below 10,000 feet.

    (b) Recovery is to be initiated before two turns are completed.

(iv) A speed of 150 mph IAS should be attained before starting to ease out of the resultant dive.

16. AEROBATICS

   (i) The following speeds are recommended:

Loop:	At least 280 mph IAS
Roll:	220-250 mph IAS
Half roll off loop:	At least 300 mph IAS
Upward roll:	300 mph IAS

17. DIVING

   (i) Speed builds up slowly in the dive and the aircraft becomes tail heavy as the speed increases. The elevator trimming tabs should be used with care.

   (ii) Care should be taken not to allow the aircraft to yaw to the right, as this produces a marked nosedown pitching tendency.

   (iii) If fitted with Bombs, S.C.I., or containers, the aircraft should be eased out of the dive gently. If fitted with drop tanks it should not be dived.

18. CHECK LIST BEFORE LANDING

   (i) Check brake pressure (100 lbs./sq.in. minm.).

   (ii) Reduce speed to 120 mph IAS and check that cockpit hood is locked open.

U - Undercarriage	-	DOWN (check green lights)
P - Propeller control	-	Fully forward
Supercharger control	-	MODERATE
F - Flaps	-	DOWN

19. APPROACH AND LANDING

   (i) <u>Approach speeds (mph IAS) at normal load:</u>

		flaps up
Engine assisted:	95	(105)
Glide:	105	(115)

   <u>Note</u>: If carrying drop tanks, bombs, or R.P., the normal engine assisted approach should be made at about 110 mph IAS.

Revised in Vol. I by A.L.42   A.P. 1564B & D. Sect. 2
and in Pilot's Notes by A.L/P   Volume I and Pilot's Notes.

- (ii) Undercarriage: The lever should have been left in neutral, but if it has been left in the UP position, be careful to disengage the thumb catch by easing the selector lever forward before trying to move it to the DOWN position, otherwise the lever may become jammed. Return the lever to neutral as soon as the undercarriage is down.

- (iii) Flaps: If 120 mph IAS is exceeded with the flaps fully down, they will be partially raised by the airflow. They will automatically move to the fully down position when speed is reduced sufficiently provided that the selector lever is left at DOWN.

- (iv) Landing with R.P. only on one wing should be made at as high a speed as possible and care must be taken to counteract dropping of the wing.

20. MISLANDING

- (i) Raise the undercarriage immediately.
- (ii) Climb at about 90 mph IAS.
- (iii) Raise the flaps at a safe height of about 200-300 feet, at a speed of not less than 120 mph IAS.
- (iv) With one 500 lb. bomb stuck up open the throttle slowly and speed on the initial climb should be 110 mph IAS before raising flaps at 120 mph IAS.

21. AFTER LANDING

- (i) Raise the flaps before taxying.
- (ii) To stop the engine, idle for $\frac{1}{2}$ minute at 800-900 rpm, then pull the slow-running cut-out and hold it out until the engine stops.
- (iii) Turn OFF the fuel cock and switch OFF the ignition.
- (iv) Check that the hydraulic selector safety plate is covering the WHEELS UP position.
- (v) Oil dilution: (See A.P. 2095 Pilot's Notes General). The correct dilution period for these aircraft is:

    Atmospheric temperature above $-10^{\circ}C$:   1 minute
    Atmospheric temperature below $-10^{\circ}C$:   2 minutes

FUEL CAPACITIES AND CONSUMPTION

(i) Fuel capacities:

    (a) Normal:

Two Main Tanks (33 gals. each):	66 gallons
One Reserve tank:	28 gallons
Total :	94 gallons

    (b) Long-range (totals):

With 2 fixed under-wing tanks (44 gallons each):	182 gallons
With 2 x 45 gallon drop tanks:	184 gallons
With 2 x 90 gallon drop tanks:	274 gallons

ii) The approximate consumptions (gals/hr.) in WEAK mixture are as follows:

Boost lbs./sq.in.	M ratio at 8,000 - 20,000 ft.			S ratio at 14,000 - 30,000 ft.		
	R.p.m.			R.p.m.		
	2,650	2,300	2,000	2,650	2,300	2,000
+4	56	50	46	57	51	47
+2	52	46	42	53	47	43
0	47	42	38	48	43	39
-2	42	37	34	43	39	35
-4	37	33	30	38	34	31

ii) The approximate consumptions in RICH mixture are as follows:

R.p.m.	Boost lb./sq.in.	Galls/hr.
3,000	+12	115
3,000	+9	100
2,850	+9	95
2,650	+7	80

23. BEAM APPROACH

STAGE	Indicated height (feet)*	I.A.S. m.p.h.	R.p.m.	Approx. Boost	Actions	Change of Trim and Remarks
PRELIMINARY APPROACH	1,500	120	2,400	-2	Flaps down 30°C	Strongly nose down
	1,500	120	2,400	-1	Lower u/c on QDR over IMB	Slightly nose down
AT OUTER MARKER BEACON	600	95-100	3,000	-4	Flaps down to 60°	Nose down
			3,000	0		Should give level flight
AT INNER MARKER BEACON	100	90-95	3,000			
OVERSHOOT	Up to 400	95-100	3,000	Full throttle	Raise u/c and retrim. Raise flap to 30°C and retrim. Raise flaps fully and retrim. Adjust boost and rpm at 1,000 feet.	Nose up Nose up Nose up

* Altimeter adjusted for Q.F.E. and touch down error as follows:
 At take-off, with no flap, the altimeter reads - 30 feet.
 At touch-down, with 60° flap, the altimeter reads -55 feet.
 so add two millibars to Q.F.E. to give zero reading at touch-down.

Note:
 The above speeds should be increased by 5 mph for Mark IID and IV aircraft.

ALSO NOW AVAILABLE!

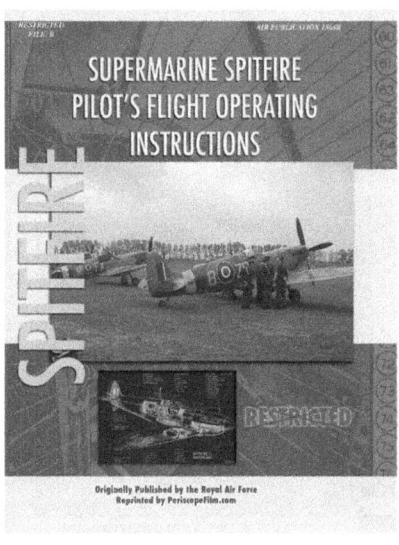
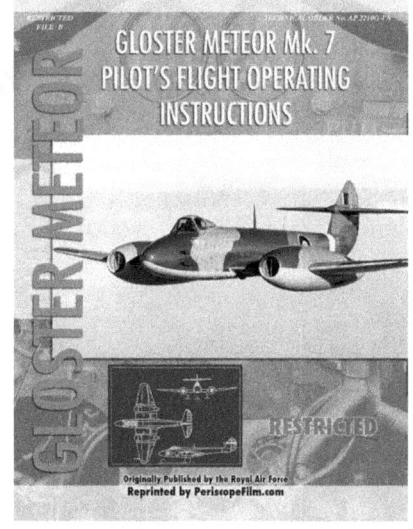

©2012 Periscope Film LLC
All Rights Reserved
ISBN#978-1-937684-75-4